Rookie
Read-About® Geography

Canada

WITHDRAWN

By David F. Marx

Consultant
Linda Cornwell, Coordinator of School Quality
and Professional Improvement
Indiana State Teachers Association

CP Children's Press®
A Division of Grolier Publishing
New York   London   Hong Kong   Sydney
Danbury, Connecticut

Visit Children's Press® on the Internet at:
http://publishing.grolier.com

Designer: Herman Adler Design Group

Library of Congress Cataloging-in-Publication Data

Marx, David F.
    Canada / by David F. Marx.
        p.   cm.   —   (Rookie read-about geography)
    Includes index.
    Summary: An introduction to the country of Canada, its
geographical features, history, people, and business.
    ISBN 0-516-21550-7 (lib. bdg.)   0-516-27083-4 (pbk.)
    1. Canada Juvenile literature. 2. Canada–Geography Juvenile
literature. [1. Canada.] I. Title. II. Series.
F1008.2.M297   2000
971–dc21   99-37402
                                                        CIP

GROLIER
PUBLISHING   1 2 3 4 5 6 7 8 9 10 R 09 08 07 06 05 04 03 02 01 00

Canada is the largest country in North America. It is also the second-largest country in the world.

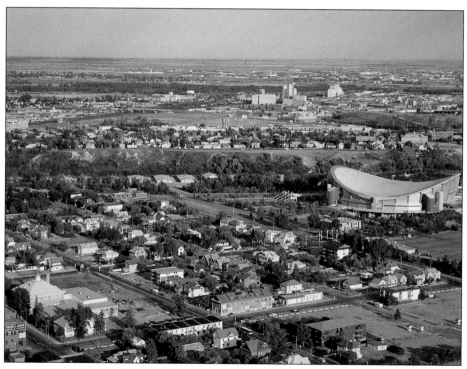

The province of Alberta, Canada

RUSSIA

ARCTIC OCEAN

North Pole

CANADA

GREENLAND

Arctic Circle

Alaska

Yukon
Territory

The Northwest
Territories

Nunavut

PACIFIC OCEAN

British
Columbia

C A N A D A

Alberta

Saskatchewan

Manitoba

Hudson Bay

Newfoundland

Ontario

Quebec

Ottawa

Toronto

New
Brunswick

Nova
Scotia

Prince
Edward
Island

ATLANTIC
OCEAN

UNITED STATES

CANADA

SCALE   1 inch = 750 Miles

0   750 Miles

0   1200 Kilometers

North

West   East

South

4

Canada is made up of
thirteen parts called
provinces and territories.

The names of these
provinces and territories
are on this map.

If you live in Canada, you need to get used to cold weather.

The land reaches north beyond the cold Arctic Circle.

Some parts of Canada are too cold and icy for people to live.

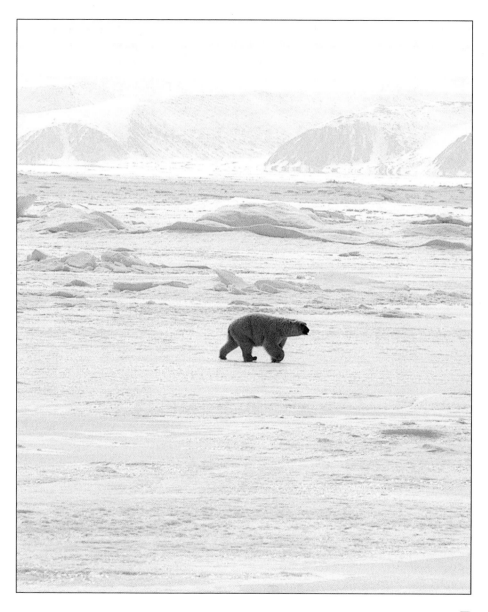

But not all of Canada is so cold. Most of Canada's 28 million people live in its big southern cities.

Toronto, Ontario

Ottawa, Ontario

Canada's capital city is
Ottawa, in the province
of Ontario.

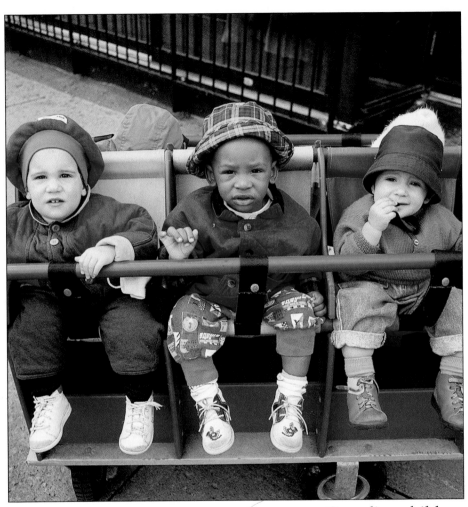

Canadian children

People who live in Canada are called "Canadians."

Many native people live in Canada. One group is the Inuit (EE-neu-eet).

Most of the people in the Nunavut (NOO-na-voot) territory are Inuit.

Inuit girls

North American Indians in Alberta, Canada

North American Indians and Inuit were the only people living in Canada before the 1600s.

Then, people from other places began coming to Canada. Most were from the country of France.

Many French people came to trade for the furry skins of animals like beavers.

The skins were used to make hats and clothing.

A lot of beavers lived along Canada's many streams and rivers.

A beaver

French restaurants in Quebec

French people kept moving
to Canada over the years.

In Quebec today, French
is spoken just as much
as English.

But in most of Canada,
English is spoken.

Canadians work in many different kinds of jobs.

In cities and suburbs, they work in places like offices, stores, and factories.

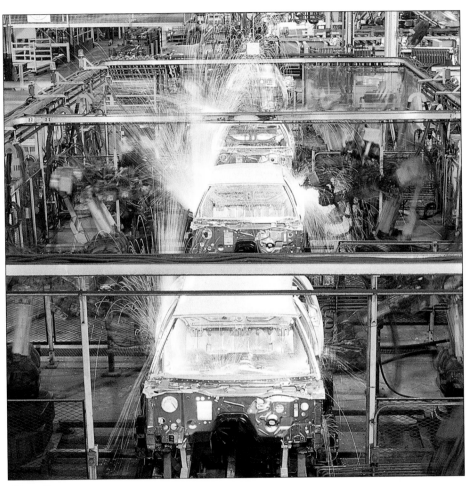

Car factory

Along the coasts, some
Canadians catch fish
for a living.

A fisher

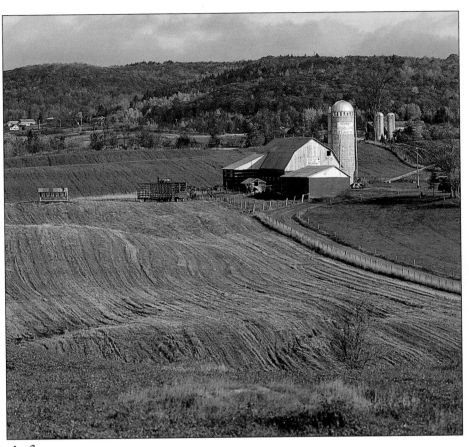

A farm

On the plains, people
farm the land.

In other parts of Canada,
people dig in the ground
to mine for oil or coal.

Mining underground

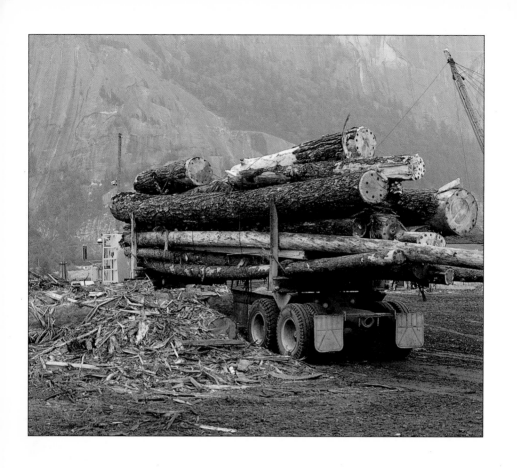

Cutting down trees for
wood and paper is another
important business.

Canada has so many maple trees that the leaf of the maple tree is on the country's flag. The maple leaf, the maple tree, and the beaver are Canada's symbols.

Maple leaves

Canadian flag

The land and weather in Canada is very different from place to place.

And Canadians live and work in many different ways.

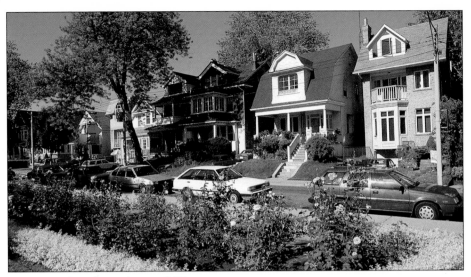

Homes in the city of Toronto

Homes in the Nunavut territory

Words You Know

beaver

Canadians

factory

Inuit

maple leaves

mine

Ottawa, Ontario

Quebec

Toronto, Ontario

Index

About the Author

David F. Marx is an author and editor of children's books. He resides in Connecticut.

Photo Credits

©: Corbis-Bettmann: 18, 31 bottom left (Dave G. Houser), 29 bottom (Staffan Widstrand); H. Armstrong Roberts, Inc.: 27, 31 top right (G. Benson), cover, 9, 31 center right (George Hunter), 14 (M. Koene), 26 (Mick Roessler); Liaison Agency, Inc.: 21, 30 bottom (Paul Souders); Peter Arnold Inc.: 29 top (Ottmar Bierwagen Photo Inc./Spectrum Stock), 7 (Fred Bruemmer), 8, 31 bottom right (Helga Lade), 25, 31 center left (Spectrum Stock), 17, 30 top left (Brian M. Wolitsky/Spectrum Stock); Robert Fried Photography: 10, 30 top right, 22 (Dewitt Jones), 3, 27 inset; Wolfgang Käehler: 13, 23, 31 top left.

Map by Bob Italiano.